For Oscar Branson
K.W.
For Lynne
A.J.

Text copyright © 1993 by Karen Wallace
Illustrations copyright © 1993 by Anita Jeram

First U.S. edition 1994
First published in Great Britain in 1993
by Walker Books Ltd., London.

Library of Congress Card Catalog Number 93–930
Library of Congress Cataloging-in-Publication Data is available.

ISBN 1-56402-303-6

10 9 8 7 6 5 4 3 2 1

Printed in Italy

The pictures in this book were done in watercolor and pen and ink.

Candlewick Press
2067 Massachusetts Avenue
Cambridge, Massachusetts 02140

My Hen Is Dancing

by
Karen Wallace

illustrated by
Anita Jeram

CANDLEWICK PRESS
CAMBRIDGE, MASSACHUSETTS

My hen is dancing
in the farmyard.

She takes two
steps forward

and one
step back.

She bends her neck and
pecks and scratches.

Her beak snaps shut.
She's found a worm.

A hen doesn't have teeth.
Food goes down into a pouch
in her body to be softened, and then
into her gizzard, where it's ground up
by the bits of grit she swallows.

My hen is rolling
in her dust bath.

She likes the ground
when it's gritty and dry.

Dust baths are good for cleaning
feathers and controlling fleas.

She cleans her feathers
with her beak and scratches
her ears with her toenails.

A hen also preens herself every day with oil.
It comes from where her tail feathers grow,
and she picks it up with her beak.

She stretches her wings
and sleeps in the sun.

My hen never struggles
if you hold her.

Her feathers are long
and smooth on her wings.

A hen can't fly far because her wings aren't strong but she can flutter up and down from a perch.

Underneath she's soft
like a feather duster.
Her bones feel hard
like thin sticks inside her.

My hen lives in a henhouse
with five other hens.

There's fresh straw on the floor

and a row
of nest boxes
along the
back wall.

A rooster lives there too. He has shiny tail feathers and a red coxcomb like a crown.

If my hen wanders,
he brings her home.

My hen lays big brown eggs.
When there are chicks
growing inside them,
she sits in her nest box
and puffs up her feathers.

She pecks you if you try
to touch them.

Some kinds of hens lay brown eggs.
Some kinds of hens lay white eggs.
No kind of hen lays both.

A hen's chicks take three weeks to hatch.
She sits on the eggs, turning them every
day so that they stay warm all over.

While she is sitting on her eggs,
she is called a "broody" hen.

Her   chicks   are   wet and

They creep underneath her

sticky   when they   hatch.

A newborn chick
needs the warmth
of its mother to
survive.

where she's fluffy and warm.

My hen leads her chicks around the farmyard.

They learn to scratch and peck

and pull worms from the ground.

It takes about six months for a
chick to grow into a hen or a rooster.

My hen knows when it's time to go to sleep.
As soon as it gets dark, she hops
into the henhouse.

She sleeps standing up.
Her long toes grip
the perch so she
doesn't fall.

Sleeping like this is called "roosting."

We close the henhouse door at night
to keep her safe from hungry foxes.

In the morning I open the door. The rooster
jumps out with my hen close behind him.

The rooster crows, and
she steps up beside him.

Hens eat all kinds of things, including corn,
crumbs, worms, insects, grass, and vegetable scraps.

My hen is dancing
in the farmyard.

The hens in this book are so busy! When they bustle around it's as if they're dancing.